# Splash!

Written by John Parker • Illustrated by Julie McCormack

The mouse jumped in.
Splash!

3

The cat jumped in.
Splash!

5

The dog jumped in.
Splash!

The sheep jumped in.
Splash!

The goat jumped in. Splash!

11

The  elephant  jumped  in.

SPLASH!

The water went out!